E

Text: Jörn Donner, Jan Mårtenson, Tor Ragnar Gerholm

Photo: Peter Gullers

Design: Olle Eksell

Publishers: Gullers Pictorial AB

SWEDEN

SE is the new national term for Sweden

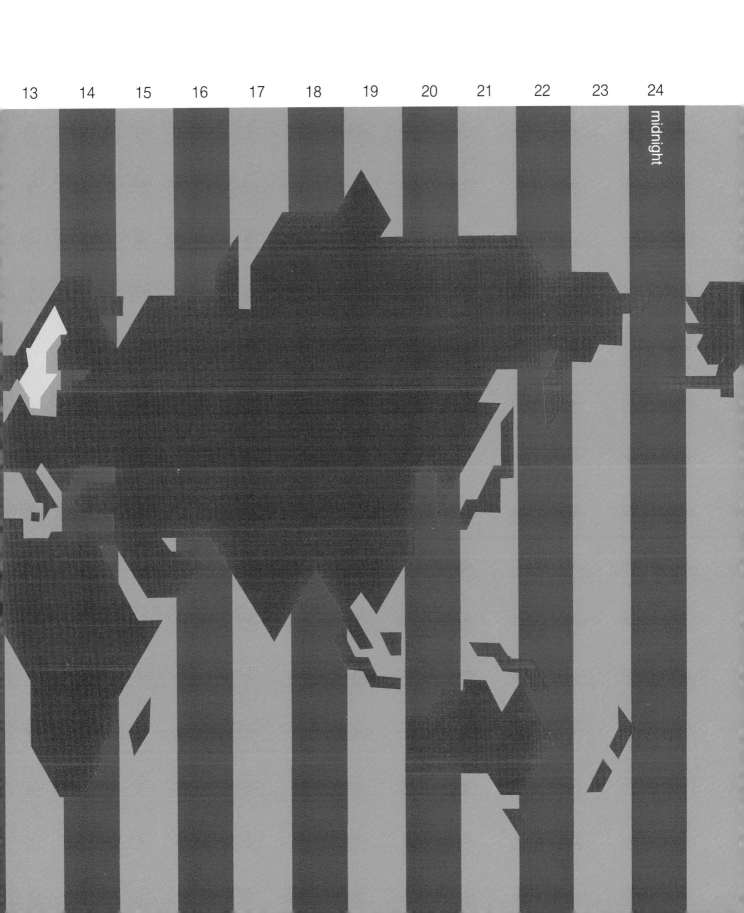

midnight

← *Sarek National Park has been called Europe's last wilderness.*
The Swedish fells cover 13% of the country's surface.

The Seven League Forest "Sjumilaskogen" at Tiveden,
in central Sweden. More than half the country is forested,
and over three quarters of it is coniferous.

A beech wood at Bökeberg, a country house in Skåne. →

Cultivated land accounts for 7% of the whole.
Less than 4% of the workforce is
engaged in agriculture; in 1950 20% was. → →

The skerries off Blekinge, south-eastern Sweden.
The coasts of Sweden and its islands
are about 13,000 kilometres long.

Jörn Donner   SWEDEN:

Is there a Swedish landscape?

Images that often re-occur in people's minds are those of Swedish meadows in summer, or Swedish woods and forests, or Swedish lakes, or coastal islands: images of Swedish natural scenery, less often of the landscapes in which most Swedes live, the surroundings of the cities of Stockholm, Göteborg and Malmö, of larger towns, in high-rise blocks or private houses, in a landscape criss-crossed by roads, power lines, and the rest of the communications network.

During recent decades Swedes have for the most part become dwellers in built-up areas, often longing for the countryside, its untouched landscapes (as they are thought to be), the scene of lengthier and lengthier holidays. A longing for the *stuga* in the country.

The everyday Swedish landscape hardly matches these images. During these decades, when millions of Swedes moved or were moved from their home tracts, the desire to "build away" urban housing shortages created many new suburbs and high-rise housing areas which are already beginning to be cleaned up: boredom and social problems were intrinsic to them, and all who could left them for private houses, either semi-detached or in their own gardens, for that was how they really preferred to live. Much inner city housing, often old and run down, was taken over by the many contemporary immigrants.

A national landscape exists but is multiform, for a single image of summer meadows fails to reflect the high-tech urban Sweden that in many ways resembles the USA, not merely superficially but also in essentials. So the images are necessarily many, none of them expressing the whole truth.

To depict a society is impossible: instead I am forced to mediate fragments, backgrounds, thoughts and images.

At the start of the 1970s, Sweden was essentially a complete or completely built society, although many contemporary politicians would have denied this, as would their successors today: politicians like to see society as incomplete, for this, at least in Sweden, justifies the reform work that all political parties say they want.

What is meant by a completely built society is a bit hard to define.

THOUGHTS AND IMAGES

Sweden as it seemed to be during the early 1970s can be sketched roughly as follows: after 40 years of effectively unbroken Social-Democratic tenancy of power, most people (including many who didn't vote Social-Democratic, the party having practically never received a majority vote) had become convinced that the party was best placed to deal with and administer Sweden Incorporated. Formally a monarchy, the country is, for practical political purposes, actually uninfluenced by the House of Bernadotte; it was imported in the early nineteenth century, when the old royal house had fallen, and now performs some important ceremonial functions.

Roads, schools, hospitals and universities existed, as well as a general social infrastructure that worked. Politicians, always politicians, would have said that there were yet roads to extend, child-care facilities, or swimming baths, still lacking – for the perfect society was yet a long way off; but by international standards at least Sweden was socially the most egalitarian society in the world.

The country's political stability matched, and was perhaps built upon, a great economic stability, and as industry was successful – it had attracted several hundred thousand foreign workers – the state's tax income rose annually and made possible an extension of social reforms. Some critics, it is true, pointed out that the state could simultaneously take control of and transfer a larger and larger part of GNP: but the answer was that the citizens of Sweden could enjoy, as the fruits of this policy, effectively free schooling and health care, and many other social benefits, including housing subsidies. Only a few critics responded by saying it had perhaps been better if individuals in Sweden could have decided more for themselves about their incomes and outgoings, for this policy could lead to the state gradually taking over and re-distributing all incomes among the country's citizens in a manner thought to be egalitarian.

So this stable Sweden met the first oil crisis in the autumn of 1973 and produced a nice example of rationalism in Swedish planning. News of a possible oil embargo, which could indirectly affect Sweden, caused rationing cards for motor fuel to be printed, and serious preparations to be made

Uppsala, the seat of one of Europe's oldest universities,
is the fastest growing "kommun" in Sweden; its present population
is 157,000. This café is open only in summer; the covered
food hall behind it is open all year. →

Medieval Week in Visby attracts thousands of tourists
to the Baltic island of Gotland.

for a crisis economy. The completely-built strong society had revealed its vulnerability to international crises: this was only to be expected, for a large part of the national welfare was built on exports and on the existence of trans-national corporations that employed abroad a growing proportion of their workforces.

During the ten years up to 1982, Sweden was not markedly changed, despite a certain amount of political drama in 1976, when the Social Democrats lost many votes, and their power as governing party, to a coalition of three right-of-centre ('bourgeois' is the usual term) opposition parties. Its policy differed only inessentially from the Social Democrats', possibly because the national concensus was deeper than many believed. Before an election (as between Democrats and Republicans in the USA) it is customary to emphasize the enormous ideological differences between Social Democrats and the bourgeois, but no large changes occured in Swedish politics from 1976 to 1982, when the bourgeois parties held power.

Most Swedes continued to regard their country as really the best possible one to live in, but might not have noticed certain long-term trends affecting it, for they might not have been apparent to those who live from day to day in the same world.

More and more Swedes took winter and summer holidays abroad, and private consumption increased steadily, despite general complaints about tax burdens. Some of these long-term trends, which were then not readily apparent, were to have some significance later.

Stenungsund is a small community on the west coast. Once the home of fishermen and farmers, it is now the centre of the Swedish petro-chemical industry, which is not Swedish owned.

A large number of oil-derived products are made there, and all the companies except a small one, Berol Kemi, are foreign owned. Berol may be owned by the Swedish state, but it is dependent for its raw materials on Norwegian interests. Although it is now constructing an ethylene terminal to permit supplies from another source, this source is Finnish owned.

While Swedish industry has become increasingly transnational, hundreds of Swedish companies have been bought up by competitors in the Northern countries or further afield. This is partly natural to an open international economy, but it does also show how Swedes have lived better and consumed more while the

17

Swedish economy has been relatively stagnant.

The unwillingness of politicians to speak openly about this led to a delayed, rather shocked awakening. Even so, I'm not altogether sure if most Swedes know how things are with Sweden, and what problems can occur in the future. Over 10 percent of those who live in Sweden were born outside the country, but far from all come from social environments wholly unlike the Swedish. Immigration from Finland, which was considerable during the 1960s and part of the 1970s but later diminished, was really a continuation of the movement from Finland that had been impelled by state power centuries ago, while Finland was still a part of Sweden.

Finnish immigrants came from social conditions that in certain respects

remind one of Sweden's, except that economic opportunities in an industrially fast-growing Sweden were greater than those in Finland, where unemployment was high.

Finnish immigrants formed the majority of immigrants in Sweden, and were less noticeable, for most of them adapted more quickly to Swedish conditions than did Yugoslavs, Greeks, Turks, Italians and Spaniards, or those who sought political asylum from the Middle East or South America.

These latter groups came from poorer social and economic conditions than those of Sweden, a materially well-off society, so one cannot blame Sweden for their arrival, even though they were a useful addition to the national workforce. They were often placed in ghetto-like living areas.

Most of them were at once entitled to the same social benefits as Swedes, and everything possible has been done to give adults tuition in Swedish-as-a-second-language, and their children mother-tongue teaching in the schools, at least during the first years.

The conventional assumption is, probably, that this 10 percent can be assimilated into Swedish society about as easily as smaller groups of immigrants from Germany, Scotland, the Low Countries and Finland have been since the seventeenth century. In other words, that the matter is not really problematic; but it is.

People have perhaps not noticed that this immigration has altered day-to-day life in a large number of Swedish communities. As numbers of foreigners grew, they became noticeable, and it became impossible in practice to overlook them as just Swedes who for some reason hadn't taught themselves Swedish. These foreign groups formed their own societies in the community as a whole.

The authorities also faced many nearly insoluble social problems: antagonism between immigrant groups, disturbances, even murder, which led to certain reactions from the Swedish side. Even so, officials have done their best to receive as many refugees, especially political refugees, as seemed possible.

The hospitality implied by this immigration was not wholly unambiguous, for the resulting population growth met the needs of large-scale industry. Things became more serious when the country entered an economic regression that was also a social crisis. Foreign workers were no longer quite so welcome on arrival, and many Swedes felt Sweden should be as Swedish as it had been.

Volvo's, and thus Sweden's, largest workplace is probably the car-production centre, *Torslandaverken*, in Göteborg. The number of foreign workers in car production has been large ever since Volvo began to expand in the 1960s.

The degree of separation between different language and ethnic groups at *Torslandaverken* is great, and efforts have been made to form work teams for Swedes, Finns, Yugoslavs, Turks. A Babel of tongues is spoken, but the official goal of assimilation is not reached. During meals and coffee breaks workers anyway form groups by language, and their pecking order is decided from the start: first Swedes, then Finns, then everybody else.

No-one can say what consequences immigration will have for Swedish society but old assumptions about assimilation no longer hold good.

Swedish urges to centralize, and for large-scale, deliberately rational operation,

A suburb from the 1960s: Bergsjön, outside Göteborg, houses
12,000 people. Nearly two fifths of them are immigrants.
Swedish and 22 other mother languages are taught in its schools.

led to the amalgamation of local government districts (communes) into units with new centres anything from 50 to 100 kilometres away from villages and small communities on their peripheries.

In practice this meant the conditions of many people's lives were greatly worsened, but these people were too few to influence or change the political decisions that had been made.

Communities were laid waste in the name of rationalism, and while remote villages could certainly enjoy the same benefits as others – school buses, health services and so on – something had been lost that could never be regained.

An example of this change is the Baltic island of Gotland, where eleven independent communes were made one, meaning in practice that 55,000 people who had good chances of directly influencing their surroundings, through a nearby local authority and its bureaucracy, had now to turn to Visby, the island's new, but for many rather remote, centre.

Sweden's best-known artist, the film director Ingmar Bergman, has returned after years of exile to Fårö, a part of Gotland and once a separate commune. Its people, less than one thousand, thus lost some part of the feelings of community they and their forefathers had built up over centuries; Bergman has depicted this in two films about Fårö, made in 1970 and 1979.

Commonsense planning can sometimes lead to nonsensical solutions, for engineering techniques cannot be equated with humanism, but this is not to say that these failures of human consideration are the work of a political party or the result of some political conviction.

The tradition of Swedish centralism is old, dating from a time long before the birth of political democracy.

The rationalism that finds expression in Swedish social planning and a well-functioning national or local bureaucracy can, when applied under other conditions, give excellent results.

Tennis is a sport enjoyed in almost all countries. Sweden stands as the foremost tennis nation in the world, not merely in relation to its population, but absolutely. Its cold climate has motivated the construction of many buildings for sports that in other countries can be enjoyed out of doors: swimming and various ball games. These buildings can be converted for other sports, among them tennis. But this is not sufficient as an explanation.

Gustaf V (born 1858) reigned from 1907 until 1950 and, like other members of the House of Bernadotte, was long-lived and tall, and a keen tennis player, often playing in winter in a tennis hall in Stockholm, still well preserved, which must be the oldest in the country. It was considered something of an honour to play doubles with him but less desirable if he and his partner were not to win. Known as 'the tennis King,' perhaps partly because he was less renowned for intellectual qualities, he often visited the French riviera and played tennis there, too, but even this cannot explain the present-day phenomenon.

Björn Borg was very young when he began to play tennis, he was 'discovered' early and soon became a star. His breakthrough came when large incomes could be won by playing tennis with the backing of sponsors. His breakthrough was helped when TV proved itself an unexcelled medium for transmitting tennis matches.

In a society not otherwise characterized by great drama, and where drama and interest could be concentrated on some event, it became almost obligatory to watch Borg's great final games, for example at Wimbledon, on TV. Most Swedes probably also approved his decision, made with taxes in mind, to move to Monte Carlo, for this was neither illegal nor morally doubtful: it is reliably believed that a large majority of the population tries to find tax loopholes, the burden of taxes being often considered too great. Unlike Borg, most Swedes could not leave the country: he, it was felt, had amassed his fortune without the help of others.

To accept the 'Borg phenomenon' as explaining later tennis successes would be to ignore the fact that Sweden was a leading tennis nation some decades earlier, and that a large number of players reached world class before the big money came into the game during Borg's time. Sweden played in Davis Cup finals, and Swedes at Wimbledon, and this tradition laid the foundations for the organized work that came to fruition after Borg.

Economic motives are plausibly behind this interest in tennis, for the incomes of the foremost Swedish players have no reasonable relationship to what, say, a university professor, a leading technologist or engineer can hope to earn. In the same way, but less intensely, football and ice hockey have acquired glamour through the hope of professional football contracts in Europe, or of entering one of the NHL arenas, although rewards there are very uneven. The new Swedish tennis stars, on average about twenty years old, are probably aware that their

Mats Wilander's home club in Växsjö (southern-central Sweden). The club has 400 junior members.

Stefan Edberg, one of the best.

Gustav Vasa laid the foundations of a strong national state in the sixteenth century.

quite exhausting careers will end before they are thirty. They dream of winning in these ten years as much honour and renown as Borg.

The real explanation of the tennis wonder, apart from Borg's example, and that of others, is the Swedish Tennis Association's net of talent scouts. It catches the finest talents in all school classes and associations, in all age groups, over the whole country, and then they get regular training and check-outs, in part at tennis camps at Båstad, in southern Sweden, with the country's best trainers. The elite is selected in a process designed to bring on world-class players among fifteen to seventeen year olds. This has succeeded during the past five years, and will certainly be as successful in the future.

Tennis and other sports can thus symbolize how well organized Swedish society is, and how its seemingly egalitarian structure can favour efforts of this sort.

Despite the presence of a large number of immigrants, Swedish society is exceptionally homogenous, perhaps because, as one of its main characteristics, it has been steered, hard, from its centre for such a long time.

When the Social Democrats came to power at the beginning of the 1930s, the party could take over and develop further a state apparatus that had long been loyal to the ruling political class, and that had several centuries' centralized direction behind it.

Historically, the Swedish monarchy has several times successfully attacked foreign powers or economic interests that could have threatened the well-being of the state. This began with Gustav Vasa (born 1496 or 1497, reigned 1523–60): he could not have been wholly displeased to have made Sweden Protestant while also contributing to eliminating the economic power of the (Catholic) church. He, and later kings, might now and then form alliances with the aristocratic grandees and the rich, but they mainly strengthened state power at the expence of others; this formed an excellent basis for the capitalistic bourgeois revolution of the nineteenth century.

Gustav Vasa thus opposed the transnational political and economic power of the Hanseatic League. Four centuries later, nationalistic defensive moves to protect the country's economic interests would be found quite compatible with overseas establishment by Swedish industrial and other interests that had reached their maximum limits within Sweden.

This national egotism, combined with a well-functioning state system, is vital to Sweden, the country having in reality been forced to accept an identity as a small state on the edge of the European continent, with national egotism as vital to its survival.

In this sense, the Social Democratic hegemony of the past five decades has directly continued the old monarchical policy, with the difference that the party has seriously tried to win the widest possible popular support for its policy. It has had to gain its democratic legitimacy by political elections held every third year, and by obtaining, at least in retrospect, the approval of a majority for what it has done.

It is really rather odd that one can speak of a genuine optimism about the future in Sweden today, despite many signs that suggest quite other feelings would be more correct.

A reliable proof of this optimism is noticeable increases, which many cannot explain, in numbers of births, while abortions have remained at an almost constant level. Some have wished, unrealistically, to attribute these increases to the immigrant population, but they are as noticeable in almost one-hundred-percent 'Swedish' districts.

A possible basis for an explanation is the regained prestige of formal and common-law marriage, which for many years had been depicted as less desirable, with traditional values once again being emphasized, and Swedish nationalism being once more legitimate. The Swedish tradition is being rediscovered.

To some extent these increases can be ascribed to the better life enjoyed by many Swedes, despite the economic troubles of the state, since 1982, when the Social Democrats regained power; this is a somewhat paradoxical development. The national economy was troubled when the Social Democrats regained power in autumn 1982: debt repayments and interest took a considerable part of budgeted income, for, by Swedish standards, the national debt was exceptionally large. While much borrowing had been internal, and so without direct effect on the balance of payments, it had depressed industrial investment, many companies having found lending more profitable than investment.

One of the new government's first actions was to decide on a 16 percent devaluation of the *krona*, which immediately gave Swedish industry a marked edge on most of its international competitors; it had previously been at a disadvantage vis-à-vis them. Since then, this positive effect has been almost eliminated, for devaluations seldom cause structural changes, being more like pills that give some temporary relief.

Together with the government's other measures of support for industry, this devaluation caused usage of industrial capacity generally to rise immediately. One should not underestimate the psychological effect of the response of state power: private industry saw itself confronted by a government with will and capable of unified power of action. The increased usage of resources then led to larger company profits, new jobs in many places, and a sense of optimism about the future, as important for economic activity as nativity.

Sweden as a whole is poised between contrasts that are often more than foreigners can understand. Private industry and commerce do very well, stock-market values rise sensationally, entrepreneurs make much-discussed windfall profits, but claims are made, abroad and in Sweden, that the country is socialistic or at any rate far down the road towards socialism!

They arise partly from the Social Democrats' verbal habit of calling themselves socialists, partly from an assumption that the strong central state apparatus must have socialized (=taken over) the greater part of personal incomes and so got unrestricted rights of decision over the individual.

This can be true for those who live mainly on various forms of social support, for sanctions and administrative decisions can easily deprive them of these benefits, but it would be an oversimplification to describe the relationship between the authorities and their clients only in this way. The phenomenon is not singularly Swedish, for people depend on such social benefits in all advanced western countries.

Yet, sometimes the Social Democratic state apparatus is obliged to take the initiative towards reforms that at least seem to be steps towards socialism, for example, the collective ownership of the means of production, which is part of an inheritance that its beneficiaries sometimes try to live up to.

For this reason, in the teeth of firm resistance from industry, commerce, and political opponents, the Social Democratic government established what may be called 'wage-earners' funds (*löntagarfonder*), funded by transfers of parts of certain larger companies' profits. There are several funds: each has certain regional connections, and each may purchase shares on the Stockholm stock market, although no one fund may hold more than a certain proportion of a company's

Customary midsummer celebrations at Tällberg, Dalecarlia.
Ulf Lundell, author/poet/rock artist, in action. →

The ski resort of Åre, in the fells.
Downhill skiing has become very popular in
recent years, thanks to Swedish successes in international competitions.

Ingemar Stenmark has now won more
than 80 world-cup competitions.

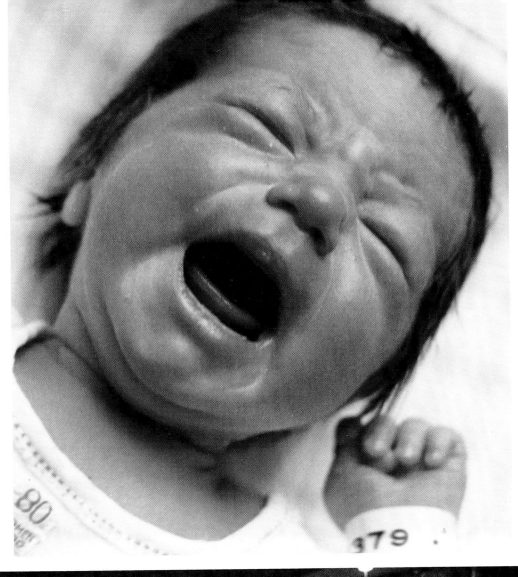

quoted share capital.

This all too evidently further increased the quoted market value of Swedish company shares, which had anyway been on the increase for a long time before these new, well-funded buyers entered the market. The reform, then, benefited either the owner/managers of substantial capital, who could see in good time what would happen, or traditional shareholders, or both groups, which had probably been among the reform's most vocal opponents.

Whether the funds can be regarded as either socialistic or a step towards socialism is highly doubtful. Although the funds are controlled, in effect, by trade union nominees, individual wage earners have hardly more chance of influencing decisions in companies in which their fund holds shares than they would as personal shareholders, whose influence in this respect is marginal.

Sweden is here a long way down the road towards Galbraith's techno-structure, an elite of managers and administrators that looks after its own interests independently of the owners; it keeps a sharp eye on the company's profits and turnover, and on the security of its own jobs.

Despite the loud protests of Swedish industry and commerce, among others, these funds will probably endure, just as the Social Democrats will probably continue to govern Sweden after the general election in autumn 1988. But it would be wrong to call this move to extend collective ownership socialist, although one can rightly talk about a step towards a corporative sort of state, with an intimate interweaving of different interests, both private and state.

In certain official circumstances, and for cosmetic purposes, the struggle between capital and labour is emphasized to suit the frame of mind appropriate to a traditional role, but in practice goverment, trade unions, private industry, commerce and finance enjoy far-reaching mutual understanding.

This is reason enough to look more closely at some of the shocks that caused changes in contemporary Sweden: the first occured in 1981–82, or before the political changes of autumn 1982.

The story of the Russian sub discovered off Karlskrona on 28 October 1981 has many farcical sides. The mass media covered the drama in minute detail during the ten days that elapsed before the Swedes pulled the sub off its bit of rock and let it proceed out to international waters. Books, TV programmes and films have been devoted to this Russian contretemps and the generally accepted interpretation holds that the boat, on some reconnoitering mission, missed an important channel and ran aground; another claims the whole thing as a genuine navigational error. Even supposing the whole story becomes known, it hardly matters what it is, for the psychological effect on the people of Sweden is really much more important, and of greater interest.

The Swedish defence chiefs knew that Warsaw Pact and NATO vessels and airplanes, as military routine, now and then tested the value of the country's defence of its neutrality. In criminal circles, it is said, nothing is a crime until one is caught.

Small infringements of Swedish air space usually occasioned no great fuss, but in this case the intruding object was large, most probably armed with nuclear weapons and, worst of all, undetected by the Swedish defence forces. When the sub was found, by a fisherman, it had been hard aground for 16 hours.

In Sweden it had long been a claim, even an axiom, within the armed forces and large parts of the population, that Sweden's defensive capabilities, in respect of its neutrality, could repel all foreign intruders. In addition, Swedish political leaders, regardless of party, had made large investments in Swedish defence technology, and it was said that, of small European countries' defences, Sweden's were strongest. But all of a sudden it was necessary to think again.

External military specialists considered, looking only to military matters, that the country had armed itself to meet armed attack, not actively to defend its neutrality.

The objective argument had less significance, for the fact of the sub itself disturbed some of many Swedes' deeply rooted habitual and conventional assumptions: neutral Sweden, wanting principally to remain outside big-power conflicts, could never attract the interest or arouse the curiosity of some foreign state. Once disturbed, they were abruptly abandoned. The enemy, now the Soviet Union, might at worst offer violence to Sweden.

This primitive pattern of responses did have some objective causes, for the strengthened role of space weapons had made Scandinavia, in a wholly novel way, an exposed position between the two superpowers.

What was important was the arousal of the Swedish people from a state of some naivety. The Karlskrona incident did not remain unique: foreign submarines were hotly pursued the following year, although no evidence was offered of their

One of three big mass sporting events in Sweden:
3,000 m upstream at Vansbro in water often less than 20°C.
The other are the Vasalopp (85 km skiing)
and the Lidingölopp (30 km running).

provenance. Proof of common ground in Swedish politics was given when Olof Palme, recently back as prime minister, won general support for his government's threat to sink, not merely warn, any such boat found in Swedish waters in future.

The grounding in Swedish territorial water of this Russian sub was paradoxical in many ways, for it happened during an international Russian peace offensive, and had effects that were surely unwelcome to the Russians: impressions of their aggressive attitudes in Europe were deepened, and Swedes became all at once nationalistic and even keener to have better Swedish defences.

Sweden is not outside, was the conclusion of this brutal awakening. But this belief had been indulged in for a long time.

"Things like this can't happen in Sweden!"

This was the popular reaction to the news that prime minister Olof Palme had been murdered just before midnight on 28 February 1986.

He was going home on foot with his wife, without any security guard, after having seen a Swedish film in a central Stockholm cinema.

Everything was very Swedish: Stockholm, even its centre with its many restaurants, was deserted, for all that the city has become something of a cosmopolitan capital.

Palme had declined a guard for the parts of his life that were private, to have a chance, for example, to see a movie without a lot of fuss.

The spot where he was killed, and its surroundings, were cordoned off, but with notable lethargy, and while the police turned out in force, and disposed of considerable technical resources, they acted too late. Very Swedish, too, for it "couldn't happen in Sweden."

Palme probably had far more friends after his death than when he was alive, suggesting that he was greatly missed. For months after his death, flowers were left every day at the spot where he died. The street nearby was renamed in his memory.

The day after the murder, queues several miles long waited to leave flowers and record their condolences at the central government offices in Stockholm.

The following morning, in bitter cold, 12,000 long-distance skiers waited for the start of the historic Vasalopp to Mora. Originating more in romance than history about Gustav Vasa, it has become one of the leading long-distance skiing competitions in the world: all these competitors stood in silence for a minute to

Youth culture: US cars, bikes, jeans
and topless bathing-suits.

commemorate him.

He was mourned differently in different parts of Sweden. Shops, stores and offices displayed his portrait, surrounded with flowers.

Memorial gatherings were held. Political opponents praised him, this in a society in which political murder had earlier been considered unthinkable.

His funeral, like that of his predecessors in the Social Democratic party, was

Tall Ships Race participants leave the harbour estuary of Göteborg.

arranged by the party, not by either the church or state: the many speeches gave little information about him as an individual, they had instead the form of challenges for the future, political appeals. Red banners and international solidarity were the dominating themes. Probably almost the whole population followed the funeral, either on the radio or TV.

Sweden seemed overcome with sorrow and national unity. The atmosphere

was reminiscent of the reactions in the USA after John Kennedy's murder, for in the USA, too, such a murder was unthinkable.

The realities were otherwise, both for Sweden and Olof Palme.

A putative consequence of the murder will be to strengthen, not weaken, the Social Democrats' future influence on Swedish society, partly because Palme's intelligence, irony and sarcasm had probably antagonised many Swedes. He had certainly been prime minister for a long time, from 1969 to 1976, and from 1982 until his death, but there were politicians, not only among his opponents, who considered his personality an obstacle to a broader degree of cooperation between Swedish political parties.

Although the Social Democrats have run the country for a long time, and so created a psychological dependence between much of the population and the party, or the organisations that support it, it has practically never won the votes of a majority. Even so, Palme was mourned by almost everyone, for all needed to participate and experience things together, to mourn in common.

Modern Sweden, materialistic in inclination and reality, can be described as a society of loneliness, for after the decline of a religion that was never especially heartfelt, nothing arose to replace it. The dominating, indeed, perhaps the only, political ideology, social democracy, had quite as eagerly as Swedish capitalism stood for a belief in a future of material progress, succeeding, even, in making it into a religion.

To faults in Swedish history, or to faulty knowledge of it, can be attributed the yearning for inspiring collective national experiences, which are missing partly because modern Sweden has developed in a manner that Karl Popper would call social engineering: the most important thing being a need for broad generally accepted solutions, even if, initially, some received the support of the smallest possible parliamentary majority. The Social Democrats had a parliamentary majority only under the bicameral constitution, which existed up to the 1968 general election; members of the lower house were elected directly, those of the upper house indirectly. But under the party's leadership, general agreement has been reached in all essential questions. One may thus call Sweden a one-party state, for this one party, never representing more than half the population, could impose its understanding of what society should be, in a way that is, strangely enough, possible only in a democracy. Despite the principle of the hegemony of the Communist Party in Eastern Europe, the ruling classes there know that their actual support is very frail, while free and secret elections in Sweden have given and will continue to give the Social Democrats the legitimacy of power.

No memorable national conflict has troubled modern Sweden, which, as a non-combatant in two world wars, could follow its chosen path towards greater social equality and substantial economic improvements for large groups, while old institutions and classes preserved their positions.

The development of Sweden over the past fifty years hardly permits dramatic descriptions. Social engineering means resolving societal conflicts with the intention of making people of equal value, but sometimes, unfortunately, it makes them just similar.

The Swedish people has a strong sub-conscious nationalism, which finds its general expression in collective participation in certain sporting successes. For individuals, it can come to light when, for example, a Swede who has moved to Switzerland returns to Stockholm to consult his doctor, for Swedish doctors are the best in the world or, alternatively, "there are no good doctors in Switzerland". But this Swede means there is no Swedish doctor in practice in Switzerland.

Without really knowing it, then, Swedes yearn for generally accepted collective experience, but the mass media are well aware of this phenomenon in everyday Swedish reality. It has caused the country to have been called a one-issue society in which a single news item or event obliterates from most people's minds everything else, of importance or not, while the dominating event somehow gets replaced by another in due course.

After late winter 1986 the murder of Olof Palme was the only news item of any importance. The entire pattern of response, of participation, sorrow and anger, seemed to mirror a long-repressed yearning for a sense of community and national unity. This is really rather odd, for Palme's own political style quite often caused splits and dissent.

The political system in Sweden, in association with the cult figures of the mass media, creates a strangely unreal atmosphere in relation to the underlying realities. One gets the impression that a few leading politicians quite simply decide what is to be done and considered, while in the same way a few industrialists (or top sporting figures) seem wholly to set the norms for economic realities (or popular leisure pursuits).

Silence, as if Palme's criticism of rulers to west or east were not needed or wrong, would have become national cowardice. An opinion, particularly if morally justified, is never wholly without meaning, but its effect must be limited: Sweden simply lacked political clout. But often, in Northern and European contexts, Swedish politicians, including Palme, have seemed to feel subconsciously that Sweden is yet the great power it was three hundred years ago. Visitors, perhaps more than most Swedes, can easily see that the country does still possess much from that time, untouched by war or invasion: the ancient university towns, the palace in Stockholm, the country mansions of the aristocracy in southern Sweden, and many large churches, to be found almost everywhere in a secular landscape.

Any small nation needs a degree of national egotism to survive, and if Sweden's, thanks to Palme's and other politicians' style, has a certain moralizing patina, under the fine phrasing things are just as nationalistic and egoistical as they need to be. When national interests have been at stake official policy has never taken a risk: for example, in preserving an export market, in further internationalizing Sweden's economy, or in making use of the world's openness while this is possible or permitted.

If the matter at issue has contrasted with some utopia, this state of affairs has obtained within the country too, where, for decades, the Social Democrats have been at once eager to act and held back by responsibility, undismayed by continuity and the high ideals of their message. The words of the Internationale, however, have scarcely been relevant here, for the workers and oppressed slaves to whom its appeal is directed now own Volvo 760s and houses, take holidays on Rhodes or by some Swedish lake, and possess holdings of shares.

The Social Democrats have striven to realize the possible, and have set its limits rather narrowly. The movement's own leaders have tried to put down attempts to introduce policies sounding too radically utopian, partly for tactical reasons. It would not look good once again, on paper, to get rid of the king and make Sweden a republic. It was easier to deprive the monarch of all real power, and instead to give the royal house enough money for resplendent ceremony: one occasion is the annual Nobel reception, which gives the world an impression of stately pomp, of continuity and dignity.

Suddenly, unwished for by all, Sweden after Palme had to adjust to a more modest role in international relations, and this is a negative proof of his signi-

A shipbuilding epoch ends as the 130m-high gantry crane is felled.
It had been used to build 650,000-ton tankers.
The site at Uddevalla will become an assembly factory for Volvos.

Korså Ironworks. A memorial of an early structural
change in the iron industry in Sweden.

Petrochemical industry in Stenungsund.

Over 3m people travel annually by car ferry between Sweden and Finland.

ficance. This adjustment began, perhaps, in 1718, when Karl XII was shot while leading a Swedish army in Norway; the immediate political consequence was that the Swedish Baltic empire, and Sweden's great-power period, came to an abrupt end. The death of Olof Palme is possibly the end of an epoch, but that is something known only to those who can be wise after the event. One cannot write the history of the future.

While a member of the goverment, Palme criticized US policy, which sometimes led to chillier political relations with the USA, while eastern European rulers were not flattered to hear him call Husak, the president of Czechoslovakia, "a creature of a dictatorship." In various connections it has been claimed that general Swedish opinion about the superpowers has changed to some extent to the disadvantage of the United States, although the day-to-day realities of Swedish life really contradict this.

No other country in Europe is probably so Americanized in its habits, patterns of consumption, films and literature, its taste in TV and music. Much of what can be seen in and around Swedish towns is reminiscent of the USA. If this could be a problem, there is little Swedish antagonism towards things American, because, in addition, the greater part of the population can use English (if seldom any foreign language).

Despite these imported habits, Sweden is well able to defend its national culture, which is attached to its language. Things would be different if, like Austria and parts of Switzerland, Sweden were bounded by another country where the same language is spoken, for then defence of a language would not be defence of a territory.

The territory called Sweden, after honourable struggles far back in time, has become self-evident to Swedes, and its defence would be self-evident, too, now that the nation, through shocks such as the murder of Palme, has been forced to see violence outside its frontiers as possible also within them. The unconscious nationalism of Swedes can thus become conscious and so stimulate fresh thinking. Any society is threatened by stagnation if it remains self-satisfied, enclosed within itself.

Göta Kanal. The canal was built between 1810 and 1832.
It has a length of 190,5 km and has 58 locks.

The bridge between Öland and the mainland is 6 km long. The
main-span has a clearance of 36 m.

DESPITE DISTANCES that are greater than in almost every other European country, Sweden functions in all essentials as a well coordinated entity. Swedes, like Swedish companies and official bodies, have no great trouble in general in reaching one another. Effective communications are a pre-condition for the Swedish way of cooperating and Sweden has for a long time now invested heavily in the different networks that, together, connect the country's scattered built-up areas. The different interests – and they do exist! – have from time to time seen one another as competitors, but most often in practice an advance for one is an advance for all: computerization has not lessened the writing of letters or personal contacts, and the telephone has not caused people to travel less.

Since the late 1970s, domestic air travel has tripled, while the number of airports has increased from fifteen to thirty eight. Year by year the network becomes all the finer and more closely integrated: the goal is for passengers to be able to reach a European destination and return home the same day.

So Swedes are slowly learning that air travel is neither particularly costly or dramatic, although for many years it was the prerogative of a briefcase-toting elite. The domestic airline, Linjeflyg, is trying, with the help of differentiated prices, to show that even private citizens can take pleasure in travelling by air. (In summer, prices in Sweden are the lowest in the world!)

When the Stockholm domestic airport at Bromma was closed, and services began to operate from relatively distant Arlanda, it was estimated that numbers of passengers would diminish. Quite the contrary! Arlanda soon had to be expanded!

Just the flight is only a part of air travel, and so domestic airports are linked with a system of limousines, taxis, buses, and even dog sleighs and hovercraft. The motto of "a thousand airports" expresses the thought that air travel should indirectly reach out to every place of consequence in the whole country.

"I'll drop it in the post this evening, so you'll get it in the morning."

One can say this with confidence in Sweden, if not in all other countries: 94 percent of all letters arrive in a day, despite the formidable distances. This means a lot for industry and commerce, for much time and expence is saved through not needing to guard against postal eccentricities. Suppliers and customers can rely on a packet arriving in two days, and the whole of industry makes arrangements accordingly.

The Swedish Post Office is effective not through technical secrets – equipment is, after all, international – but really through an attitude of mind, an unusual carefulness and good working morale, allied to an ambitious organisation. It is taken entirely for granted that all Swedish

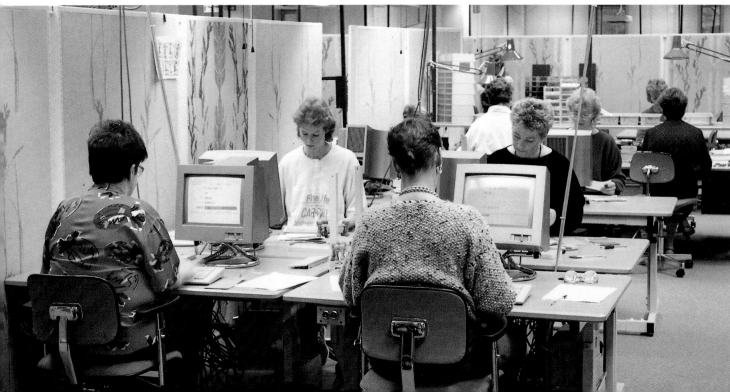

companies and households shall be well served, however remotely placed they may be on some island or in the middle of some endless forest.

The Post Office has undertaken to be the unfailing link between Swedes. This concerns overnight money transfers, too, by computer between the Postgiro accounts of official bodies, companies and private persons. The Post Office is a state-run body, of course, but is not ashamed to call itself a 'part of the business life of Sweden.'

What is it that, within a fraction of a second, connects a consultant in his car on some lonely road in Norrland with his family or a customer? Or that transmits construction drawings between an engineering company and its sub-contractors here and there in Sweden, or handles travel agents' airline bookings and the Postgiro's daily transactions that run into billions? Yes, the telephone network.

An effective, all-embracing network has been a necessity in overcomming the great distances within the country, in enabling all Swedes to communicate with one another and the world at large. With more than 900 telephones per 1,000 people, the country has the greatest density of telephones in the world. Tariffs that are internationally very low have

additionally stimulated the use of ancilliary equipment such as telefax and teletex. Today Sweden has twice as many computer connections per employee as any other country in Europe.

This has even further increased the need for telephone transmission capacity. The Telephone Administration (*Televerket*) is currently making great efforts to digitalize exchanges and to lay optical cables to meet future demands. The information-technical development that we are in the middle of may be compared in importance with the construction of railways in Europe during the nineteenth century: it is becoming a global network with unimagined possibilities.

Jan Mårtenson

Once upon a time a country's history was that of its kings. This is both correct and incorrect, right if one focuses historical development on dramatic and spectacular events in which leading contemporary personages played a decisive role. Crowned renaissance nobles, rather than poor craftsmen and farmers, were instrumental in regicide, military campaigns and sieges, but the statement is also incorrect, for an historical occasion is created by a powerful current of events and contributions that involves literally everyone alive during a certain epoch. Something that contributed to the correctness of the statement is the fact that much of the documentation that survives comes from royal chancellories and other centres of power, and touches on the great moves in history's game of chess. Another dimension of our understanding of history is that history was written by men, for it is only lately that women have been admitted to the domain of historians. Neither consciously nor maliciously, but as a consequence of a society in which women were responsible for domestic tasks, looking after the house and children, while men devoted themselves to decisive and creative functions. For this reason women's role in history has been obscured. The endless, thankless grey day-to-day work, its trials of patience, the basis for so much of development and progress, was pushed aside, to give place to feats on the battlefield, in climbing mountains, in sailing around the world and in pursuing colonial enterprises. In this respect the history of Sweden is not unique.

We may know relatively much of some of the great figures of our medieval and early modern history, but much less of their womenfolk. And we know virtually nothing at all of women at lower levels of society, especially the lowest. All these lonely women who, often under privation and suffering, maintained their homes and brought up their children. Spinsters, wives, all those who never had a chance to test their strength, borne down by conventions and prejudices. Sweden's well-being and progress have depended, it's been said, on her natural resources, iron, forests, water power among them, but I should like to add the contributions by Swedish women, womanpower. Let me give some examples.

One of the first great female figures to emerge towards us out of Swedish history is the saint, the Holy Birgitta. Her life was rich and

THE SWEDISH WOMAN

fascinating. Born at the beginning of the fourteenth century into one of
the realm's foremost families, and married when she was thirteen, she became the mother of eight children; her daughter Katarina, "the scented
lily of the virtues," was also considered a saint with her own day in *Acta
Sanctorum*. A pilgrimage to Spain was the turning point of Birgitta's life.
Some years after her return her husband died, and she settled at Alvastra
nunnery, now a ruin, in eastern central Sweden. Her divine revelations
commenced there, a glowing ecstasy against a background of medieval
daily life. Published in Latin under the title of *Revelationes*, her work laid
the foundations of her international reputation. In 1349 she left Sweden
and travelled to Rome, in an attempt to cause the papal seat to return
from its "Babylonian captivity" in Avignon, and to obtain papal per-
mission to found her own order of nuns. In the end she succeeded, and
her nunnery in Vadstena, where her grave is located, is still active today.
She died in Rome in 1373 after a pilgrimage to Jerusalem.

Birgitta's father and husband were among the leaders of her country, and
of course this greatly increased her chances of doing what interested her.
But much was demanded of her in the way of self-consciousness and strength
if she were to reach the goal she had set herself, to curb and admonish not
only her own relative, the king of Sweden, but also the rulers of England and
France, in order to bring the Hundred Years' War to an end. But she was
also aware of her faults, and prayed for release from her pride, seeing her
heart as a bladder of poison, tightly encased in a membrane of pride. "Tear
away this membrane, by which I mean pride, and replace it with humility."

In an authoritarian and patriarchal time, when women kept themselves silent
and meek in the background, the church was a male fortress, a heavy
pyramid of power, a powerful structure of cardinals, bishops, men of law
and theologians, but there could still enter Woman, thanks to Mary, The
Mother. "Where the world is betrayed by Manliness, it can be saved by
maternal power." Birgitta called her foundation "The Order of the Saviour,"
but also, "My Mother's nunnery," where religious life followed the
example of Mary, in humility, faithfulness and love.

Many centuries later we meet Kristina. A queen, talented, constantly curious,
sometimes ruthless, a "libertine," a freethinker in an epoch when,

The first and, as yet, only woman works engineer at the
Swedish Steel plant in Luleå, which is not far from the Artic Circle,
is called ELISABETH NILSSON. She is in charge of over 90 employees.

THE HOLY BIRGITTA. A rich and fascinating destiny: she
became a saint, a model for others. No-one can go further than that.

QUEEN KRISTINA OF SWEDEN. →

H M QUEEN SILVIA, an unbeatable PR figure "for Sweden in keeping with the times,"
to cite the present monarch's motto. Beautiful, charming, gifted and with a command of
several languages, she is a worthy link in the brilliant sucession of Swedish queens. →

almost as much as in Birgitta's days, a woman's place was the home and her
highest calling motherhood. Like Birgitta, Kristina had a platform for her ideas
and ideal, for she was daughter to Gustav II Adolf, the Hero of the North, who
had fought Catholicism in Europe with the bared sword of Protestantism and
died when she was six. She became queen of Sweden in 1644, at the age of
eighteen. She had been brought up under the impress of her father's instructions,
as a boy, for it was held to be something of a catastrophe that power should
devolve upon a woman. Hunting, riding and sport were on her curriculum, but
considerable intellectual demands were made on her too. She commanded all the
important European languages, she spoke French "as if she had been born in the
Louvre," and, according to a French diplomatist in Stockholm, she spoke Latin
as excellently as her native language. She was deeply interested in philosophy,
mathematics, theology and astronomy, and loved poetry and literature. In
political matters she was unusually talented, for while still young, she played off
the aristocratic grandees, whose power and privileges had grown during her
minority, against other groups, and gathered power into her own hands. And
when Sweden became "too small," she established contact with leading
contemporary intellectuals, brought Descartes among many others to her court,
and founded an academy.

But the most dramatic decision she took during her time on the throne was to renounce it and abdicate, at the age of twenty seven. She converted to Catholicism, which was something all but unspeakable: that the Queen of Sweden, the daughter of the Heroic Protestant King should become a Catholic! In Rome joy was unbounded, not least for the Pope himself, who received her with open arms. She remained in Rome until her death in 1689, but the drama of her life did not end with her abdication. In the secret agreement she had made with Cardinal Mazarin, in France, she had been promised the kingdom of Naples, but the plan was betrayed by one of her equerries, the Marquis of Monaldesco, and came to nothing. She punished him – it was one of the greater European scandals of the time – by having him murdered.

She established herself in Rome in the Palazzo Riario, enjoying a style of life in excess of that of many contemporary monarchs. She founded an academy, her palace became the gathering place for the learned and intellectuals, and her collection of manuscripts, books and art, which she had taken with her from Stockholm, and which had got there as spoils of war, was magnificent. What is left of it is now to be found partly in the Prado Museum, partly in the Vatican library, and other collections. She had her own theatre and an orchestra of which Scarlatti and Corelli were conductors. She was buried in St. Peter's, a unique honour for a convert from Protestantism. Her tombstone could well have borne the following words from one of her letters to Mazarin: "I love the storm and fear calm weather."

Many years later there stepped out into the arena of history another remarkable woman, neither saint nor political figure, but an author, Fredrika Bremer. Like Birgitta and Kristina, she was of the country's higher classes, in her case the well-to-do bourgeoisie. She was born in 1801, daughter to a wealthy factory owner. She made her name as a writer with a series of novels published in the 1830s, her work being characteristic of the new realistic school of writing. She became increasingly interested in social questions, and, in *Hertha* (1856) she took up the emancipation of women and demanded the vote for women. The book caused debate and became of great importance, and its author became one of the foremost figures in the women's movement. She expressed radical opinions with conservative overtones, summing up her position in the words "Christian Liberalism." She was active internationally, which was not so easy then as it is now, and among other work published travel books from America – *Homes in the New World* (1853–54) and *Life in the Old World* (1860–62). Her travels were not merely to enable her to see the world: she travelled to America and England to study social problems and solutions, wishing to see if they could be applied in Sweden, where she became one of the torchbearers of liberalism. Seeing clearly where armaments and distrust between nations might lead, she took part, as the Holy Birgitta had done, in the cause of peace. During the Crimean War she wrote a remarkable appeal, an invitation to an alliance of peace, which was published in England, France, Germany, Russia and America.

A close contemporary of Fredrika Bremer was Jenny Lind, the "Swedish

Nightingale." She was the finest soprano of her time and the world flocked to
hear her, for this was, of course, long before the age of TV, radio and the triumph
of the gramophone industry. Mendelsohn wrote songs for her, Hans Christian
Andersen fell deeply in love with her, and, in America, the legendary Barnum
himself was her impresario, causing her tours to be overwhelmingly successful,
artistically and economically. Prices of up to six hundred and fifty dollars were
paid for a single ticket to one of her concerts! She donated large sums to charity,
"Jenny" was entered in the Swedish calendar on 6 October, her birthday, while,
after her death, a memorial tablet was placed in Westminster Abbey to commemorate her. Another measure of her fame was the immense number of poems
about her, and dedicated to her, appearing in publications from *Punch* in England
to the *Daily Tribune* in New York. The enterprising Mr. Barnum characteristi-
cally promised a prize of no less than two hundred dollars for the best poem on
the theme of "Greeting to America," which was to represent Jenny Lind's feelings
on landing in America, and which she was to sing at her first concert in New
York. He was rewarded with seven hundred and fifty three works, and the com-
petition was declared to have been won by Bayard Taylor, a young poet and
journalist, who was later to become United States ambassador to Germany. As a
sample of the adulations of the poetical choir, *A Sonnet to Jenny Lind*, published
in *A literary and musical journal*, begins:

> Enchantress of the North! thy Silver songs
> have floated to us over the sounding sea
> Like perfumes from the groves of Araby.

The woman writer who won most fame is Selma Lagerlöf, the lonely, poor
schoolteacher who was plagued by lameness throughout her whole life. Her genius
and creative power, however, caused her work to be read, and her person loved,
all over the world. She died in 1940, at the age of 92, having been the first woman
to be awarded an honorary degree by the University of Uppsala, the first woman
to be elected to the Swedish Academy, her innumerable honours being crowned
with the award of the Nobel Prize for Literature.

She came from Värmland, a province of folktales, tall tales and story tellers,
a part of Sweden where many great writers have been born and received their
early inspiration. She grew up on a small property, in the company of women,
loving her father, a reckless extrovert who was incapable of dealing with money
and unworldly at a time of economic depression in Värmland, so that much of
what he undertook failed, while he himself took to drink, and in the end lost
his property. It was a trauma for the young girl, who never really got over it
until, late in her own life, she could use her royalties to buy her beloved Mår-
backa and rebuild it so that it came finally to realize her dreams of the place as
it had been of old. There, in the kitchen and the maids' rooms, she had grown up
in this countryside of bards and sagas, whose tales had formed the foundation for
her own work.

Her books reflect a humanistic ideal, in which people are ennobled through
moral improvement and sacrifice, the tension between good and evil, and how
God ultimately presides over the fate of mankind. She often wrote about lonely

women, and she held the formal speech at the great congress for women's rights to vote. Personally I gained an insight into her international greatness when a United Nations ambassador explained to me how his first journey after the Second World War from his home in Asia was undertaken to Värmland, Selma Lagerlöf's countryside. For several years during the war he had been forced to remain hidden in the jungle, where the only literature was a translation of Selma Lagerlöf's collected works. Reading the books time and again, he became so fascinated that he decided he had to see with his own eyes this landscape she had described. No author can do better than that.

One of those who helped to transfer her books to the screen was another Swede, Greta Garbo, that star of the first magnitude in the cinematic heaven. She acted in no fewer than thirty films, and succeeded in moving from silent films to the talkies, something that not all actors managed. Her first big part was in Lagerlöf's *The Saga of Gösta Berling*. Some years later, in 1925, she arrived in Hollywood, where her career as an actress reached its peak in *Anna Karenina*, *La Dame aux Camelias*, and *Ninotchka*. She chose to retire from her artistic achievements, and to live withdrawn, detesting publicity. This has contributed to the myth of the Divine Garbo, the inaccessible, the ultimate prey of journalists and photographers. But she still arouses lively interest, her films are shown, and some years ago she was honoured with the award by the King of Sweden of the Order of *Nordstjärnan*, symbolically named the Star of the North.

Swedish women have also played leading roles on the political scene, and fore-

← ←

Children's books, plays and films have spread all over the world from ASTRID LINDGREN'S writer's den. Small children and large have come to love her work, which has been published in more languages than one can really keep track of. "I write to please the child within me and can only hope in that way that other children can have a little fun," she says. As if she hasn't succeded! MARIT PAULSEN, an eager debater, deeply-engaged in environmental questions, and a writer. She is now a farmer, fighting for the survival of country activities being throttled as a consequence of modern techniques. She was born in Norway. Arlanda is the largest airport in Sweden and one of the largest in Europe. Women occupy three of the most important posts there: BARBRO FISCHERSTRÖM is airport chief for the National Civil Aviation Administration, HELLE KONGA-NIELSEN is Station Manager for SAS, and INGRID SANDKVIST is in charge of the customs' administration; each is responsible for a large staff of employees.

INGA-BRITT TÖRNELL, a lawyer, is ombudsman for equality, and so has responsiblity for ensuring that politicians' fine words about greater equality between the sexes are realised in working life and also protect the weak there against discrimination.

KERSTIN SIRVELL has been voted 'businesswoman of the year.' She is a dynamic civil engineer and boss of KabiGen, a sophisticated research-and-development company specializing in gene techniques and cell growth.

An interest in people and training, plus a chance to live an open-air life, led KAJSA LANDERHOLM to apply for entry to the skerries battalion of the Swedish coastal artillery. Her training began when she started her military service in 1984; its first stage was completed in autumn 1987, when she became a second lieutenant.

SISSELA BOK, a researcher at Harvard University, is best known for her remarkable moral philosophic study, Lies. She is married to Derek Bok, President of Harvard University. She is the daughter of two Swedish Nobel prize winners, the economics professor, Gunnar Myrdal, and the Nobel peace-prize winner, Alva Myrdal, a politician and disarmament negotiator.

most among them was, until her death in 1985, Alva Myrdal. Some years earlier she had been awarded the Nobel Prize for Peace, the most splendid of her many international honours. She had begun her career as a teacher in Stockholm and became more and more involved in questions of birth control and women's rights. Together with her husband, the internationally celebrated economist, Gunnar Myrdal, like her a Nobel laureate, she wrote *Crisis in the Population Question*

(1934). The book came to play an important role in directing and building up Swedish welfare policy. Her activities in Sweden were followed by international work: she was director of the United Nation's Department for Social Questions, then of a department of UNESCO. In 1955, she became Swedish ambassador to India, where she established a close contact with Nehru, and was involved in the programme of social development for the under-privileged countries. She became Swedish Minister for Disarmament, and the chief Swedish delegate at the Disarmament Conference in Geneva; she took the initiative in founding the internationally celebrated Swedish International Peace Research Institute, where I had the pleasure of working with her. She made herself known not least for her strong criticism of the great powers' policy about nuclear weapons, which is well expressed in her remarkable book *The Game of Disarmament*. In 1980 she was awarded the Einstein Peace Prize; according to its charter, it is to be awarded to persons who, following the spirit of Albert Einstein, have contributed significantly to the avoiding of nuclear war and to strengthening peace, by their example and by what they have done. This citation sums up her aims and life's work, which other Swedish women, such as the ambassadors Inga Thorson and Maj-Britt Theorin, are following today.

I have thus given a few examples of women in Sweden who have succeeded in reaching their goals, who could make contributions in virtue of their talents and independence. I have chosen and displayed some vivid lives and fates – but many others could have been named too, women who contributed in other fields, women of different backgrounds who came from other classes of society, who lived in other times. There is something that unites them all: their vision, their will and their struggle to realize their ideals. But what of the others, the patient mass of anonymous women who formed the foundation for and background to the deeds of men? Those who, despite a strong will, great talents and knowledge, could never develop themselves or their ideas? Here, happily, a pleasing change has taken place during our lifetimes, perhaps more quickly in Sweden than in many other places. Swedish legislation gives women at work rights equal to those enjoyed by men; an *ombudsman* is responsible for seeing that this law is enforced. A person who discriminates against a women in questions of employment and promotion can be fined, while employers are required actively to promote equality of the sexes by means of planned, deliberate efforts. There are already many precedents, which shows that those in authority do not wield their swords in vain in questions affecting women.

Since the early 1960s, a new development has taken place in working life in Sweden: increasing numbers of women, not least married women, have gone out to work, and in 1983 the figures of men and women aged between 16 and 54 who were at work was 86% and 78% respectively. This figure for women is equivalent to almost 50% of the workforce, although it should be borne in mind that almost 45% of women, but only 6% of men, work part-time. In addition, while women in Sweden enjoy the right to work in all categories of jobs, including the defence forces, there are in practice two work forces, one of men and the other of women, being characterized not least by differences in pay. Furthermore, women's contributions are concentrated in relatively few sectors, mostly in service and health-care jobs, while 99.5% of all top jobs in the private sector are occupied by men.

Even if much has been done to establish equality for women, the ancient hoary truth remains, that women must work hardest, because they are responsible for home and children. But a change in attitudes is on the way, not least among younger people. It is supported by legislation: for example, a man now has the right to paid free time on becoming a father, so that he may remain at home for certain periods to look after his child. And the pattern of education has been changed for the better: in 1983 more than half first-year students at Swedish universities and places of further education were women. But much remains to be done. Today's sisters of the Holy Birgitta and Queen Kristina must carry on the struggle, but we men – or at least most of us! – are on your side, making the light at the end of the tunnel a little brighter. Keep up the fight, girls!

STINA EKBLAD came to Sweden from Finland via Denmark. She is the new star in the Swedish theatre, and she also works in film and TV. She has played "Antigone" and "Julia" and has filmed with Ingmar Bergman.

Tor Ragnar Gerholm   THE

W e Swedes have been called the Japanese of Europe, and national GNP *per capita* really has grown quicker in Sweden than anywhere else in the world, except possibly Japan. In 1870 Sweden was a starving needy under-developed country, and a hundred years later it found itself to be one of the richest in the world, perhaps the very richest. To our dismay we discovered that we lived in a society of excess, and strange as this may sound, the discovery was no unalloyed pleasure: on the contrary, many found it a real 'future shock.'

During the 1970s vociferous successful protests were made about most things: against economic growth, against environmentally destructive production, against the waging of war by the United States in Vietnam, against nuclear energy and against the balance of terror. The splendid projects and 'future planning' of the social engineers lost their gloss, and eagerness for reform, a little like Hamlet's resolution, became sicklied o'er with the pale cast of second thoughts. The forerunners of new projects rather lost their breath.

E ven Swedes may need to recall that when the Second World War ended in 1945 Swedish industry was uniquely well placed to expand. The country's production apparatus was undamaged and in relatively good condition, and out in the world what Swedish industry could supply was in just about unlimited demand: wood and paper products, iron ore and steel. Domestic supplies of electricity were got by exploiting rivers unmercifully, without anyone protesting about the protection of nature. The countryside emptied as small farmers and farm workers left the land in streams, women went out to work, and the country accepted what was, for Sweden, a considerable degree of immigration.

B etween 1950 and 1970 Swedish industrial production doubled, larger Swedish companies successfully established themselves on world markets, and Sweden became one of the few countries to own multi-national companies. Swedish assets abroad exceeded foreign assets in Sweden.

Even if post-war preconditions were in fact exceptionally good, such successes are not won without hard deliberate work, and in the longer term perhaps the most valuable acquisition of these record years was the costly experience gained by Swedish industry and commerce, both at

ALLENGER CHALLENGED

home and abroad. In any event, by the middle of the 1960s things were changing, although this was not observed at the time: the market for capital goods began to be saturated, while gradually iron and steel were replaced by aluminium, polymers and fibreglass. The Swedish and European infrastructures began to be completed, railways' expansion stagnated and many lines were closed, and motorways were no longer being built as intensely as before. Housing construction slowed down too.

As a result demand shifted from raw materials and semi-finished products to increasingly sophisticated goods. This was something serious for Swedish industry, for the wholly dominating part of the country's exports comprised raw materials or scarcely processed products. This was troublesome not just for industry: the country's successes on the world market had been a precondition for the rapid advance in material conditions within the country, which expressed itself largely in an increased consumption of imported goods, and a constantly increasing stream of charterflight holidays to sunnier countries to the south. In a word, Sweden had become highly dependent on the world around.

Years of toasts to the future had induced a state from which there was a sudden awakening: the oil crisis of 1973 showed all too clearly just how vulnerable the Swedish economy had become. Almost overnight a healthy surplus on the balance of payments became an enormous deficit that wouldn't go away for years, and accumulated into a severe foreign debt. By 1985 interest alone amounted to almost 3% of GNP, or a tenth of export incomes, a sum as large as that required for the defence budget.

But that wasn't all: the secondary and tertiary effects of the rise in oil prices affected large parts of the economy. Swedish shipbuilding yards had done extremely well on the world market through high quality and efficient production, but their speciality was supertankers, the demand for which vanished as oil prices rose, and the crisis was almost at once acute. Much the same thing struck Swedish shipping lines, and almost as hard.

And when the shipyards got into difficulties, so did the iron and steel industry, and then in turn the mines, which lost domestic customers, while increased transport costs, a direct result of rises in oil prices, made it

75

all the more difficult to compete on world markets.

Other industrial countries suffered, too, naturally enough, but Sweden was more vulnerable than any other, thanks to the special structure of her industry, and to the fact that *per capita* oil consumption was the highest in the world. And all that on 100%-imported oil!

But not everything can be blamed on the world around us. Unemployment that in almost all other countries followed the oil crisis was something that we, faithful to our welfare ideology and labour-market policies, tried to eliminate through state initiatives. The result was a very weak development of efficiency, and at the same time the public sector expanded. In 15 years it grew from one third to two thirds of GNP, or proportionately twice the volume of other OECD countries. On top of that pay increases pushed up labour costs by over 40%.

This has naturally resulted in a large, low-productive do-it-yourself activity, and a rapidly growing grey economy.

But dependence and vulnerability found other, non-economic, forms of expression, for the Swedes became aware of their exposed geopolitical situation through the repeated, and sometimes dramatic, infringements of their territorial boundaries. These culminated when the celebrated Soviet submarine was found to have run aground outside the supposedly well-guarded marine base in southern Sweden at Karlskrona. Less dramatic, but more insidious, has been the steady fall of acid rain, contaminating tens of thousands of Swedish lakes (there are close to eighty-five thousand of them) and watercourses, and rendering many sterile. There is no real shortage of domestically-produced contamination, but there's no doubt that most of the sulphuric contamination comes from the continent and the British Isles. There had been radioactive fallout during the 1950s, but that from Chernobyl came as a real shock, reaching Sweden before any other west European country, and so putting the country, for once, right in the forefront of an international catastrophe. Even the Three Mile Island accident, for all that it set off violent political debate, and contributed to the overthrow of a government, and left national energy policy in disarray, had not done that.

The country's dependence on the world around has showed up in mass culture, in literature and the arts, with a demographic expression in a clearly growing contribution from immigrants in what had previously been, ethnically speaking, an extremely homogeneous population. People didn't only come to Sweden, for

During the last decade the Swedish steel industry has completed a thorough structural rationalisation. Swedish Steel, Domnarvet has specialised in sheet steel for the engineering industry.

many left the country too. Most, naturally, left as tourists, but there was a straightforward emigration of especially highly educated specialists, top management, professional sportsmen, and artists. Not so many in numbers, perhaps, but a remarkable brain-drain nevertheless.

What had stood as an example of astonishing economic successes and industrial triumphs on the world market, a small, neutral, alliance-free country that had shaken its oratorical fist at the great powers and fearlessly spoken on behalf of other small powers, suddenly found its economy in trouble, its borders infringed upon, its integrity threatened! The challenger had been challenged.

Has this little country a future, as a small country? Those who live here live in a country that has gone from almost complete independence to an almost un-

←Paper is still one of the country's most important exports.

*The Ortviken newsprint mill is the world's largest producer
of TMP (thermomechanical pulp). ASEA has developed an
integrated system for automatic regulation and control of
the mill, the power supply and the machinery.*

*ASEA equipment in one of the energy company Jämtlandskrafts control rooms.
Modern control equipment for power stations are based on
microcomputers, which opens new possibilities to optimize the operation,
increase the safety and utilize the natural resources in a better way.*

Indalsälven Power Station. There are few industrial countries in the world for which hydro power has been equally important as in Sweden. One important factor for the development of the basic industries has been a very low price for electric energy, which today contributes with about 50 % of the total production. Thanks to hydro power Sweden has one of the lowest prices for electricity in the world.

Vattenfall's wind-power research station on Gotland.

controlled dependence on the world around for its economy, renewal of technology, and social and cultural life. Never before, at least in modern times, have
Swedes felt that they have to adapt to what goes on outside the borders of their
country, and there is a widespread fear, justified or not, that this can cause
Swedes to lose control over their country.

One thing is undebatably clear in all this: a precondition for the country's independence and integrity is necessarily, if not wholly, the vitality and dynamism
of its industrial, commercial and financial activities, while its industries must be
internationally competitive.

Back to reality

The adventurous social experiments of the 1960s, and the wide-ranging societal
debates of the 1970s, pale before the sorrows and troubles of economic adversities.
Experience has shown that there are no simple remedies for structural problems.
It becomes necessary to be literally radical with the causes of trouble, and not
to put off doing what's necessary, even if it hurts. The question is to reestablish a
belief in the future, and a climate that smiles on innovation, which is in itself
essential to continued success on world markets. It is less easy now than during
the 1950s and 1960s, when rapid economic growth brought technical development with it. Other stimuli are necessary now: taxation and other fiscal reforms
to increase savings and accessible risk capital, state support of a new, flexible
and unbureaucratic sort for R & D, technical solutions and cooperation across
existing boundaries in large development projects, and, in them and in general,
dynamic management, and skilfull economists, technicians and marketing people.

If we haven't already got that, we're well on the way to getting it. Thanks to
a series of surprisingly successful devaluations the *krona*'s value has been reduced
by 40% and so brought into line with the world market. In less than 10 years
our earlier extreme dependence on oil has been halved, and diminished oil prices
and shrinking dollar rates had (up to early 1987) cut our oil bills. The balance of
trade is no longer negative, Swedish industry is working at high pressure and is
looking into the future hopefully towards a continued high level of international
demand.

Much of the structural change that competitor countries have yet to go through
is behind us, the country's shipyards having been so successfully put to rights
that the Japanese have sent a delegation here to see how we did it. The iron and

steel industry has been rationalized and acquired new, more refined products, and the volume of ore production has been adjusted to world market demands, so that mining looks as if it can be profitable again. The paper and pulp industry has been making its oil and raw materials go further, in part by substituting thermo-mechanical pulp for chemical, partly by shifting production to more refined products.

Slowly but surely the country's industry is changing from its earlier total concentration on raw materials and semi-finished products, with an unmistakeably clear development towards more refined goods. The iron and steel industry is going in for special steels and other novelties, including composite materials, and ceramics, and new production processes. The mechanical industries are using NC machines, automatic processes and robots to increase efficiency and production, Sweden now possessing the world's highest density of robots. At the same time the introduction of CAD/CAM techniques is in widespread active preparation.

The car industry has a special place in the country, and while Volvo and SAAB, even together, are minute by international standards, they are more profitable than much larger competitors. Each produces much more than cars, and Volvo alone accounts for almost 12% of Swedish GNP. The national car industry is right out ahead in matters of technical development and efficient production.

Swedish management had early on seen that transport and distribution were rapidly developing areas of technology, but out of custom rationalization has usually been concentrated on production, for no better reason, perhaps, than that in early industrial development production costs amounted to over 80% of the total. Much more was to be gained there than in distribution, but by the 1950s production and distribution costs were about equal, while the latter now account for some 75% of the total.

So, with this background, it's satisfactory that the country's car industry should have done so well with trucks and trailers, and that ASEA and SJ, the state railways, should now be working jointly on a rationalized system of track distribution. Much more can be expected as the advanced methods in use in production are applied to transport techniques.

Materials handling within companies has become increasingly important in making the best use of capital, and in the mechanical industries there is an advanced use of automatic trucks, pallet lifts, and computer-controlled high-level cranes.

Oskarshamn Nuclear Power Station.

The Svalöf Plant Breeding Company. Its breeding and research work
is aimed at producing types of grain that give bigger
yields and have greater resistance to disease. Thousands of sorts of
the same grain must be analysed before the required qualities are found. →

In 1983 the 150 kV direct-current cable was laid between
Gotland and the mainland. It is 90 kilometres long.

Context Vision, a company that is a spin-off development from
Linköping University. The company develops computers and
systems for automatic image processing. This is a rapidly growing
area with many applications, including medical diagnosis,
urban planning, metalurgy and astronomy. An ordinary
photograph of stars before and after image processing.

International communications and distribution will be greatly eased, not just for Sweden but for the whole Scandinavian peninsula, once the bridges over the Sound and the Belt (10 kilometers between Sweden and Denmark, and 20 kilometers within Denmark, respectively) have been built. Like the Channel Tunnel, they have been exhaustively, even exhaustingly, discussed by generations of visionaries.

Distribution comprises much more than just transport: packaging, storage, and marketing, and a number of initially small companies, Tetrapak and IKEA are two examples, have developed their ideas and grown large on them, becoming in the process multi-national.

Despite all the political discussion and debate it has generated, Swedish energy policy has worked really quite well, electrical energy being cheaper in Sweden than in almost every other country, and a clear advantage for Swedish industry internationally. The national grid is extensive and reliable but the referendum decision, from 1980, to have done with nuclear energy generation by 2010, is already casting its shadow on the present: half of Swedish electrical power now comes from nuclear power stations! This wind-down will probably lead to an increased import of fossil fuels and an increase in the price of electricity. The development towards a greater use of electricity, and thus higher efficiency, is at risk. Certain industries are likely to be hard hit: ASEA-Atom, the only company outside the great powers that can offer ready-built nuclear power stations, can be obliged to break off its internationally acclaimed development of SECURE, its new, small and safe nuclear power plant.

Whatever happens in Sweden, electricity consumption out in the world is certain to continue to grow, ASEA's pioneer work with long-distance transmission of electrical energy, for example with high-tension direct current, most certainly has a bright future.

Swedish distribution and communications cannot be mentioned without naming L. M. Ericsson and the national telephone administration, and their many years of developmental work; one result of it is the AXE telephone system, one of the most advanced in the world, and, we hope, destined to come into widespread international use. One promising sign has been the successful import of the idea of spin-off development of university research, and there are now small lively groups closely associated with the universities, where, in effect, research papers in many different subjects are being treated as blueprints

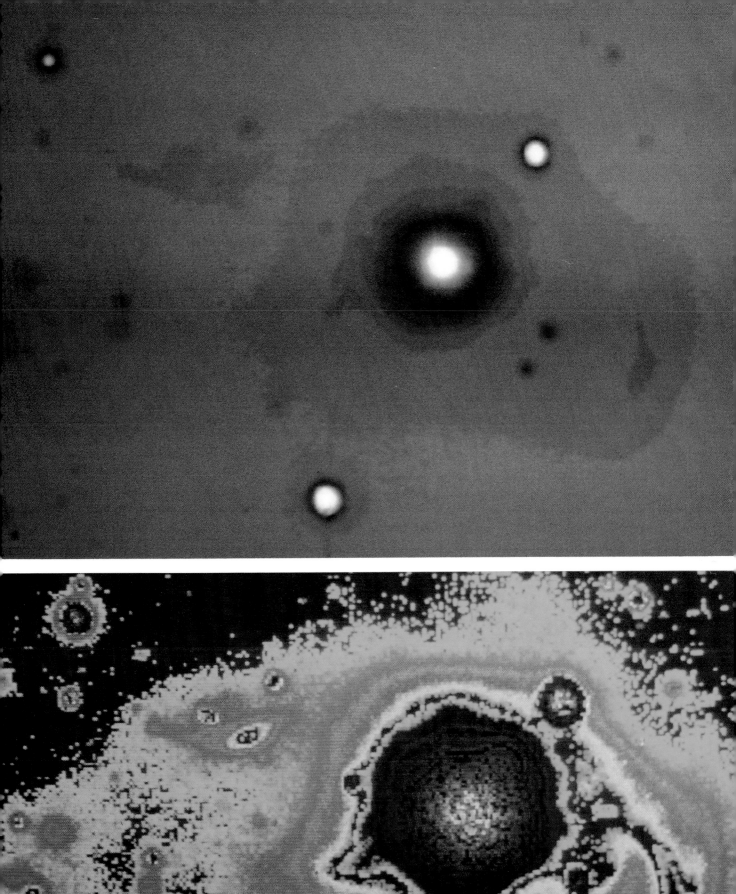
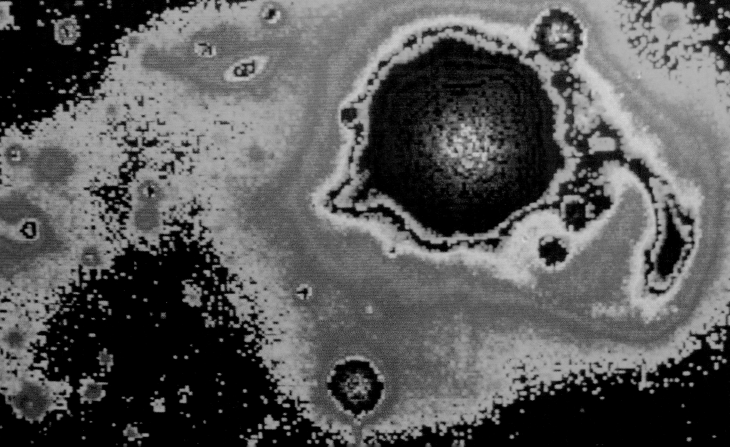

for commercial development of promising ideas and research results.

Swedish medical-products companies established themselves early with successful products such as the blood substitute, Dextran (Pharmacia), and the local anaesthetic Xylocain (Astra); other drugs, for heart conditions, for example, and a growth-hormone drug to eliminate dwarfism, which has been developed with the help of gene techniques, are carrying on this tradition. Medical technology has produced commercial successes, including knee and thigh-joint prostheses, artifical kidneys and pacemakers. Development is still going on with respirators and mechanical hearts, and with titanium implantations for false teeth and prostheses. Medical photography entered an unexpected dimension with the international recognition of Lennart Nilsson's talents.

In the service sector Swedish contracting firms, among them Skanska and ABV, have grown large and established themselves on the international scene, thanks to a combination of skilful planning and projects management with exemplary quality control. A pleasant reward for hospitality to political refugees has been the introduction into Greece of the Swedish postal numbering system: leading figures in the present Greek administration worked as postmen in Stockholm during the junta years in Greece.

Early Swedish emphasis on raw materials and semi-finished products left consumer goods relatively neglected, but who has now not heard of Hasselblad cameras? Or seen Bergman's films? Or heard ABBA's music or musicals? Something of a contrast is a company that began life making clocks and watches and

Mölnlycke's automatic goods handling, using driverless trucks, from BT Industries AB.

which has grown into ABU-Garcia AB. Its products, multiplier reels, rods and
other fishing tackle, are appreciated in Scandinavia and the rest of Europe as
ABU, and as Garcia (the name of its wholly-owned subsidiary) in north America.
Other consumer goods and the like include artist-designed and handblown glass,
from Orrefors and Kosta, and ceramics from Gustavsberg and Rörstrand.

Industrial development in Sweden since the depression of the 1930s owes much
to the extraordinary Marcus Wallenberg, the banker, whose talents for selecting
potential top management are now proven: many large Swedish groups are now
in the hands of men whom he chose and trained, and they, in their turn, are
continuing the tradition. The space left after his death in the early 1980s has
afforded room for new figures: P. G. Gyllenhammar has a unique position as leader

of the Volvo Group, and among other new finanical figures, Anders Wall has become an important factor in the national economy.

Do we look after our human capital with an eye on the future? Swedish scien-
tists and technicians take part in international research projects, in CERN, the
centre for the most advanced research into elementary particles, and in ESO, the
international astronomical observatory in Chile for the southern hemisphere.
Swedish participation in the inter-European research programmes, ZET (fusion)
and EMBL (molecular biology) is at a high level, a Swedish professor, Lennart
Philipson, being head of the latter. Sweden is also a participant in the EUREKA
programme.

Contact with the international research world is excellent, as could be expected

Ten years ago, the Swedish car factories were considered to
be too small to have any possibility of survival,
but rationalised production, high quality and technical
innovations have enabled them to carve out a niche.
The SAAB 16-valve motor has become a contemporary leader of style.

Computer technology enables individual cars to be identified on Volvo's assembly line.
The possibility of combining a large number of
different alternative components has made this necessary.

SAAB's Linköping factory: the 340 passenger airplane has been developed in conjunction
with the American Fairchild Corporation. Production has been wholly taken over by SAAB.

Basic research at Pharmacia. Closeness to Uppsala University
is meaningful for exchanges of knowledge and
recruitment of qualified people.

Guest lecturers from Thailand at the Faculty of Veterinary Medicine
of the Swedish University of Agricultural Sciences, Uppsala.

Cell and molecular biologists at Umeå University do research
in conjunction with the medical drug company, Kabi.

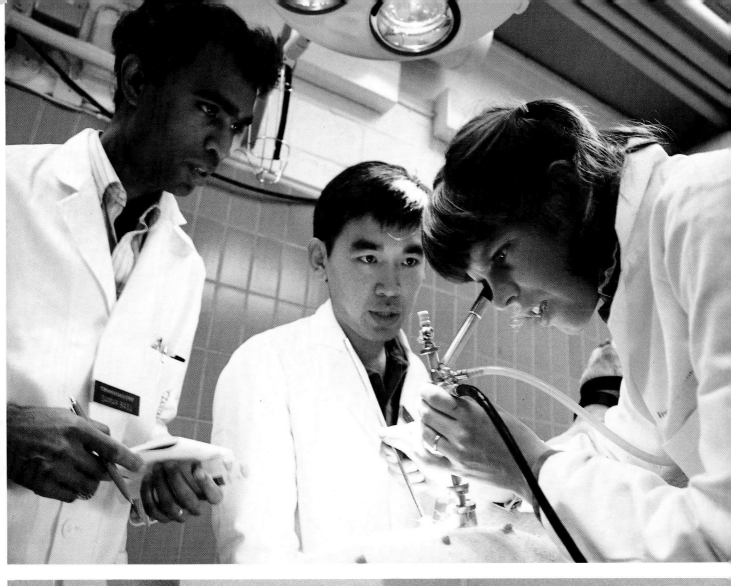

if only as a consequence of the information gathering that is the foundation for the Nobel prize awards in the sciences. At home, however, things are not so good, for the combination of urged-on reforms and economic stagnation through the 1970s has left its mark on education: higher education and research has been starved of funds, younger researchers see their careers stunted, and their and their families' lives restricted, by poor pay for short-term research projects. Technical maintenance of heavy equipment has been neglected for too long, while technical and administrative services are hard to get and of poor quality when available.

Applied research, not always of the very best quality, has expanded at the expense of basic competence, and in many university subjects it is now difficult to recruit professors and to organize satisfactory research education, in particular because those who might otherwise continue their studies, and their research, are attracted by high pay in industry which cannot be matched within higher education.

At least it seems now generally accepted that something must be done, and among the first who have received the latest signals are the students themselves. This isn't so surprising: increasing numbers are trying to get into mathematics, natural sciences and the technical and economics faculties, and we must hope we can offer these new students and younger researchers much better conditions in future.

In 1984 I made a brief survey of trends of development in Swedish society: "I believe," I explained in conclusion, "that the hitherto rapid development towards increased material welfare, a better environment and an increasingly rich life in the arts will slow down . . . . I believe that more or less confused assumptions about 'a new view of the world' will quickly spread, giving nourishment to anti-intellectualism, superstitions, religious fanaticism and general nuttiness, but at the same time there will be a fresh respect for the sciences, for educating art, literature and music, as well as technical knowledge and manual skills within different sub-cultures, that will more and more consciously and successfully guard their independence and their integrity."

Today I feel convinced that it is these sub-cultures that hold Sweden's future in their hands. In other words, I am cautiously optimistic: this small nation, despite everything, really does have a future.

The new student-union building of Stockholm University contains
a bookshop, cafe, lecture halls and much else.
It was designed by Ralph Erskine, a Scot architect who has
practised in Sweden since the 1940s.

*The annual presentation of the Nobel prizes takes place
in the Concert Hall in Stockholm on 10th December.*

*His Majesty King Carl XVI Gustaf hands over the 1986 Nobel Prize
for Medicine to Rita Levi-Montalcini from Italy.*

Sweden

Constitution	Constitutional monarchy
Head of state	King Carl XVI Gustaf, b. 1946
Parliament	One House, 349 members

Sweden covers 174 000 sq. miles (450 000 km2) and, in terms of land area, is the fourth largest country in Europe. Sweden has a population of 8 358.000.

Population

Largest cities	1986
Stockholm	663 217
Göteborg	429 339
Malmö	230 056
Uppsala	157 675
Norrköping	118 801
Örebro	118 443
Linköping	117 835
Västerås	117 732

Foreigners living in Sweden

	1960	1970	1980
Totally	199 000	412 000	389 041
Of these are from			
U.S.A.	2 000	6 000	6 374
Chile	–	–	9 238
Denmark	30 000	31 100	25 105
Great Britain	2 000	4 000	8 939
Finland	75 000	209 000	138 622
Greece	23 000	21 000	9 397
Italy	5 000	8 000	4 409
Yugoslavia	1 000	37 000	38 409
Norway	20 000	28 000	26 445
Poland	–	14 000	15 455
Turkey	–	4 000	21 105
Germany	2 000	6 000	11 972

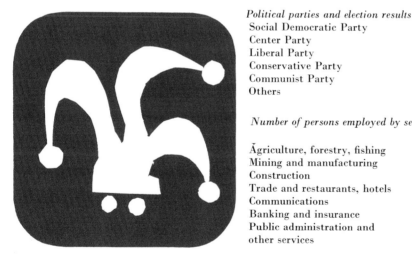

Political parties and election results	%1979	%1982	%1985
Social Democratic Party	43,6	45,6	44,7
Center Party	24,1	15,5	12,4
Liberal Party	11,2	5,9	14,2
Conservative Party	15,8	23,6	21,3
Communist Party	4,8	5,6	5,4
Others	3,7	3,8	2,0

Number of persons employed by sectors	1985	1976–84	1985
	1000's	*Annual change %*	
Agriculture, forestry, fishing	208	−1,9	−5
Mining and manufacturing	1 024	+0,8	+1
Construction	260	−1,1	−0,4
Trade and restaurants, hotels	591	−0,4	0
Communications	300	+1,2	+1,7
Banking and insurance	321	+4	+1,7
Public administration and other services	1 594	+2,8	+0,7

Education

Elementary education. A 9-year compulsory comprehensive school starting at the age of seven. English is compulsory from the third year. French or German offered as a second language. Certain options from the seventh year. The "*Gymnasium*", corresponding to Senior High School in the United States, covers 2-4 years. It offers education and training on both theoretical and practical lines, and is a merger of the traditional Central European "gymnasium" and the former vocational school.

Universities have existed in Uppsala, Lund, Gothenburg, and Stockholm for a long time, but there is also one in Umeå and one in Linköping, and a number of colleges on graduate level throughout the country. The number of students has grown rapidly — from 50 000 in 1963 to 125 000 in 1985.

Adult education has great traditions in Sweden, and courses are offered along every possible line, nowadays also through TV. Many adult education schemes are offered by organisations like the Labor movement, the Temperance movement, churches, etc.

Native language education is offered both pupils and adults in more than 60 languages.

Standard of living

Swedes take access to the countryside largely for granted, thanks, really, to the country's low population density: outside urban areas it is very low indeed. The customary law, *allemansrätt*, imposes only restrictions that are predictable by the visitor: don't enter enclosed land; don't damage crops or anything growing, either in what you do or how you drive; don't litter or risk uncontrolled fires. Don't drive on private roads. Nuts may not be picked but on unenclosed land you may pick wild berries, mushrooms, fungi and pine cones. Leave protected species of flowers alone (see posters outside tourist informtion offices etc.).

Take care in the shooting season (elk, deer), in the nesting season (the country attracts birds and ornithologists in myriads), by fishing waters (rights are widespread), and in northern Sweden (reindeer are shy). Leave your pets at home: anti-rabies rules are properly fierce. Otherwise camp where you like for up to 24 hours, swim, boat, bike, walk, ride or ski more or less anywhere, and drink from springs, streams and lakes. If in doubt (camping a second night, skating, private fishing, shooting season, edible fungi and the like), ask. Have a nice day.

Economic standard	1975	1980	1985
Key figures			
GDP SEK 1 000 *per inhabitant*	30,8	62,9	103
Consumption of paper, kg	195	205	222
Passenger cars *per 1 000 inhabitants*	336	347	377
Telephones	661	796	890
TV sets (licenses)	354	380	390
Consumption of electricity, GWh	10,9	11,3	15,6

Technology and Research

The wealth of Sweden depends largely on technological and scientific skill - past, present and future. Major questions pertaining to scientific research are handled at cabinet level by the Research Council, with the Prime Minister as chairman. Commercial and industrial interests dominate goverment-sponsored projects, however: by 60% to 40%, in terms of money.

Some Swedish inventions

Screw propeller	John Ericson (and Francis Smith)	1836
Safety matches	Gustaf Erik Pasch	1844
Dynamite	Alfred Nobel	1867
Steam turbine	Gustaf de Laval	1889
Wrench	Johan Petter Johansson	1892
Milking machine	Gustaf de Laval	1896
Zipper	Gideon Sundbäck	1900
Automatic sun valve (for lighthouses)	Gustaf Dalén	1906
Spheric ball bearing	Sven Wingquist	1907
Refrigerator	Baltzar von Platen—Carl Munters	1918
TetraPac	Erik Wallenberg—Ruben Rausing	1944
Xylocain (local anaesthesia sedative)	Nils Löfgren—Bengt Lundqvist	1948

Transportation

Registered automobiles (passenger cars)	1986
Volvo	980 232
Saab	453 675
Volkswagen	323 198
Ford	297 202
Opel	291 874
Mercedes Benz	120 833
Toyota	102 761
Mazda	100 917
Audi	80 337
Fiat	73 894
Renault	62 149
BMW	51 432
Peugeot	49 453

Industry Sweden's largest companies

Company	Turnover SEK M 1985	Total employed
Volvo	86 196	67 857
ASEA	40 199	60 979
Electrolux	39 688	93 624
Ericsson	32 496	74 692
Saab-Scania	31 840	45 181
KF	29 622	29 712
ICA	25 274	12 250
SKF	19 963	44 265
Sabaföretagen	19 843	17 176
A Johnson & Co.	19 800	5 980
SAS	19 790	29 730
Nordstjernan	17 633	22 491
Televerket	15 495	43 537
Skanska	14 951	28 219
Vattenfall	14 756	11 787
Stora	13 089	17 718

Export *Largest export industries*

Company	Main products	Total sales abroad SEK M 1985
Volvo	Cars, trucks, buses, earthmoving and construction equipment	29 842
Saab-Scania	Trucks, buses, cars, aircraft, heat exchangers, control systems	19 946
Ericsson	Telephones, telecommunications equipments	13 877
ASEA	Electric equipment and machinery, power plants (also nuclear)	10 694
AB Electrolux	Vacuum cleaners, refrigerators, freezers, washing machines	7 806
Stora	Paper	6 531
Sandvik	Special steels, alloys	4 972

Foreign trade *by groups of commodities*	Exports SEK M	1985 %	Imports SEK M	%
Foodstuffs, beverages	7 219	2,8	14 945	6,1
Raw materials	26 179	10,1	10 765	4,4
Timber	9 565	3,7	1 887	0,8
Pulp	9 627	3,7	–	–
Ores	4 729	1,8	3 773	1,5
Mineral fuels	12 736	4,9	46 226	18,9
Chemical products	16 236	6,2	26 751	11,0
Manufactured goods	67 631	26,0	36 704	15,0
Paper, paperboard	25 283	9,7	2 706	1,1
Iron and steel	17 109	6,6	8 154	3,3
Non-electrical machinery	38 609	14,9	22 200	9,1
Electrical machinery	28 850	11,1	31 073	12,7
Transport equipment	41 224	15,9	21 330	8,7
Various finished goods	21 301	8,2	30 187	12,4
Shoes and clothing	2 328	0,9	11 682	4,8
Instruments	4 817	1,9	4 775	1,9
Total	259 985	100	243 978	100

Foreign Trade *by countries 1985*	Exports SEK M	%	Imports SEK M	%
EFTA	50 971	19,6	40 339	16,5
Norway	27 208	10,5	14 730	6,0
Finland	14 671	5,6	15 941	6,5
EEC	112 499	47,1	131 635	54,0
Denmark	21 482	8,3	16 534	6,8
Fed. Rep. of Germany	29 918	11,5	43 618	17,9
United Kingdom	25 708	9,9	34 361	14,1
Other industrial countries	59 004	26,7	39 757	16,1
USA	30 143	11,6	20 445	8,4
Japan	3 507	1,3	12 001	4,9
State trading countries	8 588	3,3	13 529	5,5
Soviet Union	2 664	1,0	5 607	2,3
Developing countries	28 924	11,1	18 719	7,7
OPEC countries	9 051	3,5	4 647	1,9

Demand and production

GDP, by use	1985	1975–1984	1985
	SEK 1000 M	Annual volume change, %	
Private consumption	436	+0,5	+2,6
Public consumption	237	+2,5	+0,9
Gross investment	164	−0,2	+6,5
Private sector	77	+0,3	+12,5
Public sector	51	+0,1	+1
Housing	35	−0,6	+2,5
Change in stocks	5		+1,1
Exports	303	+4,5	+2
Imports	284	+1,4	+8,1
GDP at market prices	861	+1,4	+2,1

GDP, by sectors	1985	1974–1984	1985
	Share %	Annual volume change, %	
Agriculture, forestry, fishing	3,7	0	−3,2
Mining and manufacturing	24,8	+0,4	+3,8
Electricity, gas waterworks	3,4	+6,9	+3,8
Construction	8,1	+6,9	+3,2
Private services	35,4	+1,4	+1,7
Public services	24,6	+2,8	+1,7
GDP at market prices	100,0	+1,4	+2,1

The budget

The Central Government expenditure	SEK M 1986/1987
Royal Household and Residences	34
Ministry of Justice	10,008
Ministry for Foreign Affairs	10,673
Ministry of Defence	26,368
Ministry of Health & Social Affairs	84,491
Ministry of Transport & Communications	11,994
Ministry of Finance	18,413
Ministry of Education & Cultural Affairs	41,488
Ministry of Agriculture	6,567
Ministry of Labour	19,583
Ministry of Housing & Physical Planning	17,623
Ministry of Industry	9,860
Ministry of Public Administration	4,000
Parliament and its Agencies	470
Interest on National Debt, etc.	71,000
Unforeseen expenditure	1
Total voted expenditure	332,575

Medicine

Sickness benefits vary from 8 to 446 SEK a day, according to income, and are subject to taxation.

Doctor's fees are refunded in full or in part, as well as expenses for transport in many cases.

Prescribed medicines: maximum 55 SEK.

Industrial Injuries Insurance covers all employees, and includes a daily sum, payment for disability, and compensation to dependants in case of death. For *childbirth* every mother is guaranteed 18 months' leave of absence, an outright premium, free dental care, and daily allowance according to income. The father is permitted to replace the mother with compensation equal to sick benefits.

Hospitals are administrated primarily by county councils and are of a very high standard. The cost for medical care is 50 SEK.

Free medical examination is available to pregnant women, mothers and infants, and to pre-school children. (Regular check-ups are compulsory in school.)

Dental care is free for school-children, and available at a reduced charge to adults.

Glasses are subsidized for children and young people up to the age of 19.

Religion

The church of Sweden

was firmly established as an Evangelical-Lutheran church in 1593. All Swedish citizens are members unless they have withdrawn formally or were born to parents who do not belong. Members of independent denominations are frequently members of the Church of Sweden as well. Since 1958 women can be ordained as ministers. Since 1982 the Swedish Church has a central government of its own.

Members of the Swedish Church in 1985	7 629 762
Members of Independent denominations	
Pentecost Movement	100 323
Swedish Missionary Society	79 880
Salvation Army	32 599
Evangelical National Missionary Society	23 870
Swedish Babtist Church	21 095
Örebro Missionary Society	22 322
Swedish Alliance Missionary Society	13 553
Jehovas' Witnesses	12 151
The Roman Catholic Diocese	116 101

The Nobel Price

Swedes who have been awarded the Nobel Prize

1903	Svante Arrhenius	chemistry
1908	Klas Pontus Arnoldson	peace
1909	Selma Lagerlöf	literature
1911	Alvar Gullstrand	physiology or medicine
1912	Gustaf Dalén	physics
1916	Verner von Heidenstam	literature
1921	Hjalmar Branting	peace
1924	Manne Siegbahn	physics
1929	The Svedberg	chemistry
1929	Hans von Euler, b. German	chemistry
1930	Nathan Söderblom	peace
1931	Erik Axel Karlfeldt	literature
1943	George de Hevesy, b. Hungarian	chemistry
1948	Arne Tiselius	chemistry
1951	Pär Lagerkvist	literature
1955	Hugo Theorell	physiology or medicine
1961	Dag Hammarskjöld	peace
1966	Nelly Sachs, b. German	literature
1967	Ragnar Granit, b. Finnish	physiology or medicine
1970	Hannes Alvén	physics
1970	Ulf von Euler-Chelpin	physiology or medicine
1974	Eyvind Johnson	literature
1974	Harry Martinson	literature
1974	Gunnar Myrdal	economics
1977	Bertil Ohlin	economics
1982	Sune K. Bergström	physiology or medicine
1982	Bengt I. Samuelsson	physiology or medicine
1982	Alva Myrdal	peace

Sport

Sport is part of Swedish way of life, and the state-subsidized Swedish Sports Confederation (Sveriges Riksidrottsförbund) has about 2,5 mill. members and about 2 mill. of them are believed to go in for sport and exercise on a regular basis.

Soccer and ice hockey dominate among the ball games, followed by handball, basketball, and bandy, similar to land hockey but played on ice. Athletics (track and field) is widely spread — there are more than 3 700 athletic fields in all. Sweden has more golf courses than any other European country outside the British Isles.

Gymnastics has been a compulsory subject in schools for generations, and series of "keep fit" programs on TV have activated over a million people.

"Vasaloppet", an annual 53-mile ski race, is the biggest in the world — around 10 000 people usually take part.

History

500—600	The Svear emerge as the most powerful tribe.
800—1050	*The Viking period.*
	Swedish Vikings control the seaways to Constantinople and make trade expeditions to the Orient and Western Europe.
830	The first Christian church founded by Ansgar, a Frankish monk.
1050—1532	*The Middle Ages.*
1164	The first archbishop takes office.
13th cent.	Finland conquered in crusades. New provincial laws written, unique in Europe in age and content.
1397	Nordic Union formed under Danish leadership to fight Hanseatic League.
1521	Swedish rebellion against Danish superiority ends in victory under Gustav Eriksson Vasa.
1523—1721	*The Vasa period. Sweden as a world power.*
1523	Gustav Vasa crowned. Builds up an administration, and restores the economy by confiscating Catholic Church property.
1611	Gustavus Adolphus, his grandson, ascends the throne. Promotes municipal self-government, science, education, mining, and the arms industry. Further expansions east of the Baltic.
1631	Gustavus Adolphus defeats the Catholic Confederation at Breitenfelt, dies at Lützen the following year.
1648	End of the Thirty Years' war. The Treaty of Westphalia brings Sweden large areas of northern Germany and makes her a world power, supported by France.
1654	Queen Kristina abdicates and is converted to Catholicism.
1654—1697	Further expansions and increasing military power but the economy under great strain. Charles XII king in 1697 at the age of 15.

1700—1721	The great Nordic war begins when Denmark, Saxony-Poland, and Russia under Peter The Great unite to defeat Sweden. Charles the Twelfth killed in 1718. End of the Swedish empire.
1721—1818	*A period of domestic expansion.*
1723—1772	Constitutional government and a strong parliament, in which four estates (nobility, clergy, burghers, and peasants) are represented. Two political parties emerge. Freedom of the press 1766. Progress in science, agriculture and industry
1772—1792	Gustavus III makes bloodless revolution to restore royal power in 1772, encourages culture. Assassinated during a masked ball in 1792.
1803	Beginning of land reform aiming at integration of split farm holdings.
1808—1809	War with Russia puts an end to Swedish supremacy over Finland.
1809	New constitution adopted.
1813	Alliance with Great Britain. Swedish troops help defeat Napoleon at Leipzig under Jean Baptiste Bernadotte, former French general.
1818—1918	*End of wars, Modern era begins.*
1818	Bernadotte becomes king of Sweden and Norway. Neutrality is the guiding principle of Swedish foreign policy.
1840's	Decade of liberal opposition among new class of merchants, factory owners, etc.
1842	Elementary schooling made compulsory.
1850—1930	More than a million Swedes emigrate to North America.
1880's	Trade unions formed. Temperance movements, feminist movement, beginning of co-ops.
1889	The Social Democratic Party founded.
1905	End of union with Norway.
1914—1918	Sweden neutral during World War I.
1918	*Democracy and non-alignment.*
1918—1921	Universal suffrage for both men and women.
1920	The first Labor administration.
1921	Capital punishment abolished.
1957	Social security program (ATP) adopted after referendum.
1976	After 44 years, the Social Democrates has to hand the ruling of Sweden to a Government consisting of three non-socialist parties.
1982	The Social Democratic Party takes back the ruling of Sweden.

Other photos:

Front leaf KW Gullers,

p. 24, 31, 101 Pressens Bild,

26, 46, 50 Björn Enström

31 top Tiofoto/Sven Gillsäter

38 Bilsport, 45 top Drottningholmsteatern,

43 Tiofoto/P O Stackman, 51, 85, 89 Thomas Wingstedt,

52 bottom, 53 SAS, 64 top Nationalmuseum,

65 Åke Sandin, 66 Georg Sessler,

87 ASEA, 100 Per-Erik Svedlund

Printing: Tryckcentra AB, Västerås

Type Composition: Tryckeri AB Björkmans, Eftr

Paper: 170 g Macoprint

© Gullers Pictorial AB, 1987

ISBN 91-86440-24-1

The Esrange space research centre is located above the Arctic Circle.